LEE EVANS ARRANGES CONTEMPORARY CHRISTIAN FAVORITES

P9-DDF-725

ISBN 0-7935-6822-6

HAL•LEONARD® CORPORATION

7777 W. BLUEMOUND RD. P.O. BOX 13819 MILWAUKEE, WI 53213

HOW BEAUTIFUL

Words and Music by
TWILA PARIS
Arranged by LEE EVANS

Flowing (circa ♩ = 104)

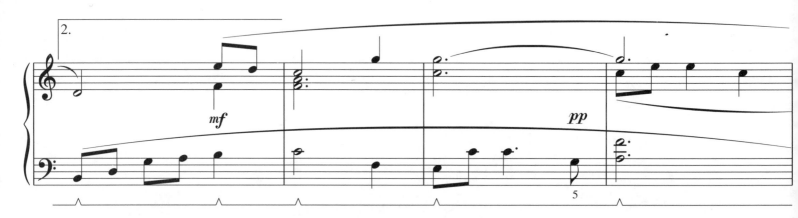

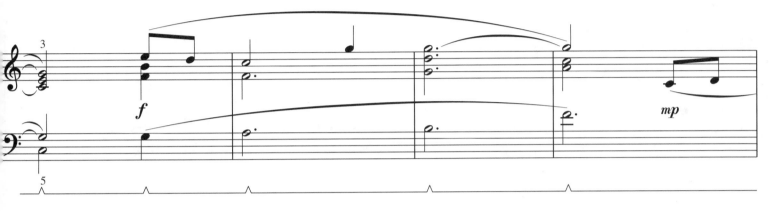

D.S. al Coda
(with repeat)

To Coda

CODA

4

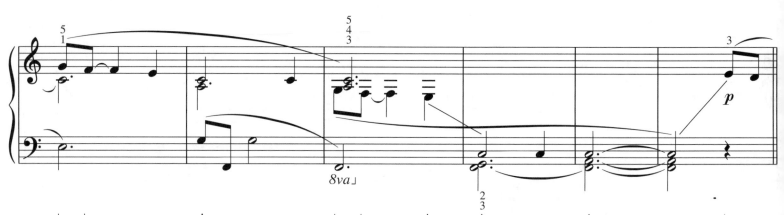

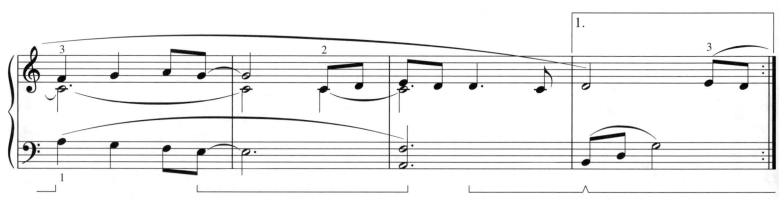

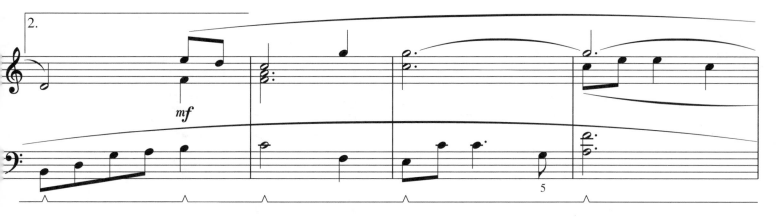

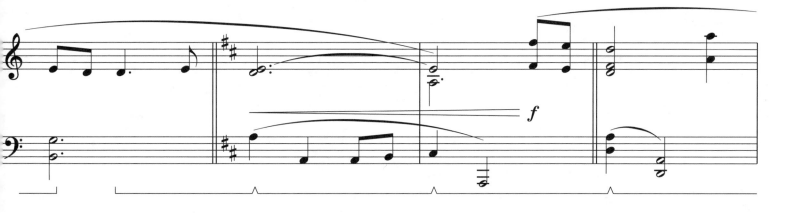

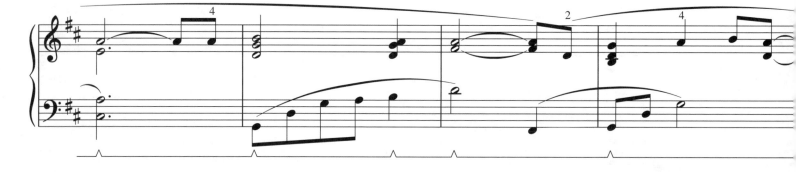

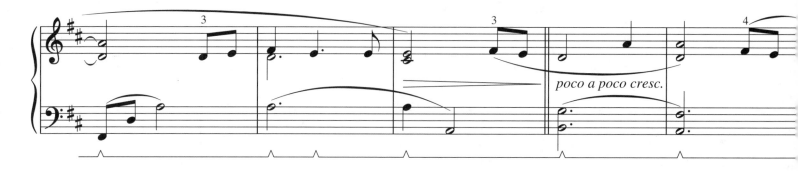

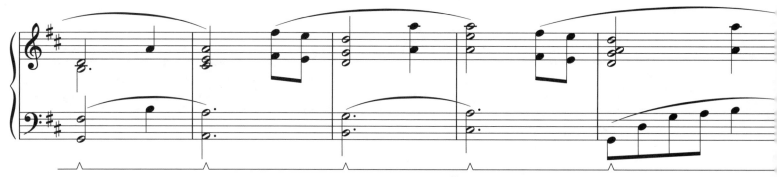

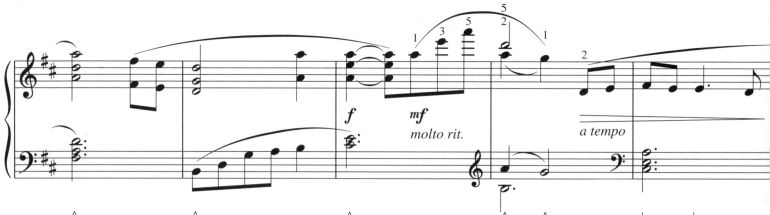

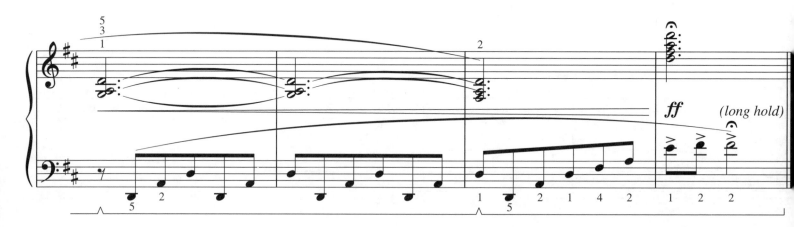

MAJESTY

Words and Music by
JACK W. HAYFORD
Arranged by LEE EVANS

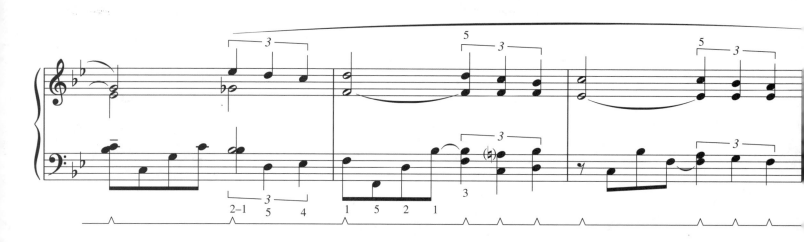

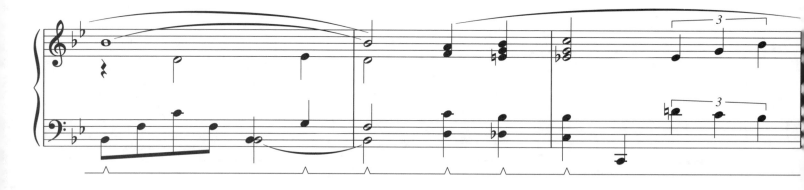

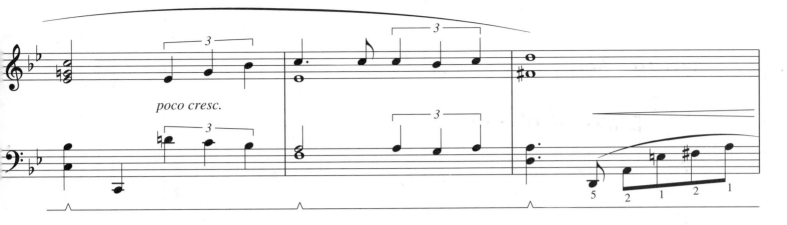

poco cresc.

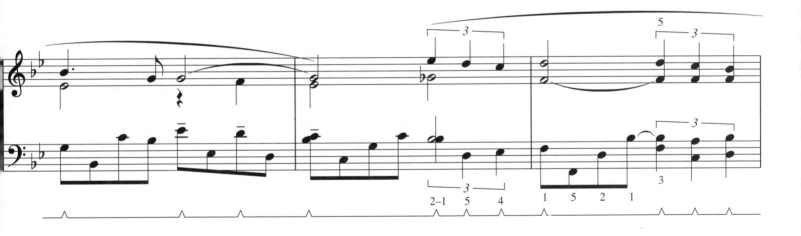

molto rit.

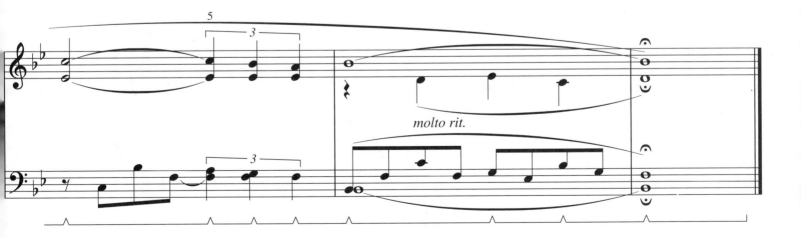

CELEBRATE THE CHILD

Words and Music by
MICHAEL CARD
Arranged by LEE EVANS

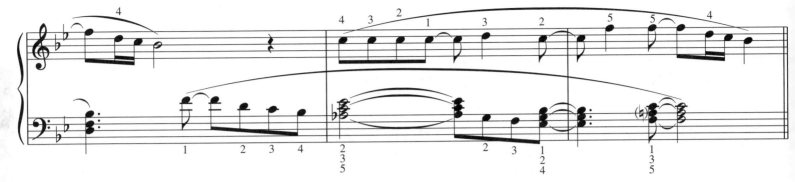

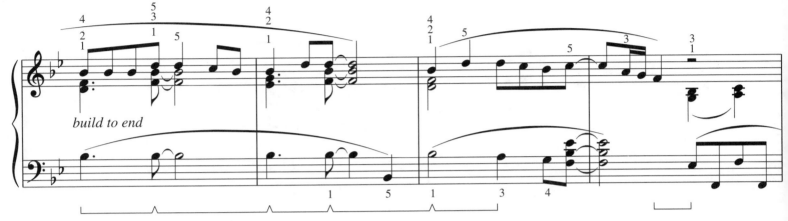

build to end

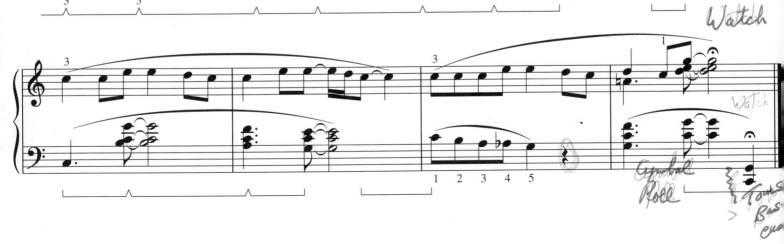

build to end

Watch

ONLY JESUS/CALVARY'S LOVE
Medley

Words and Music by PHILL McHUGH
and GREG NELSON
Arranged by LEE EVANS

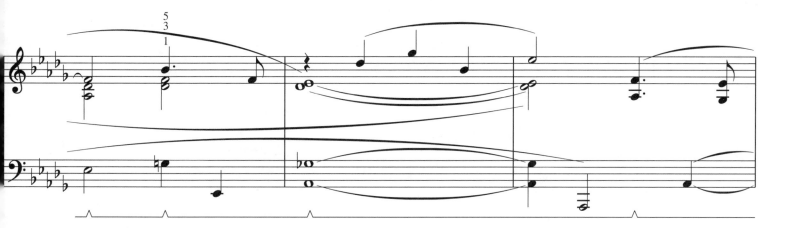

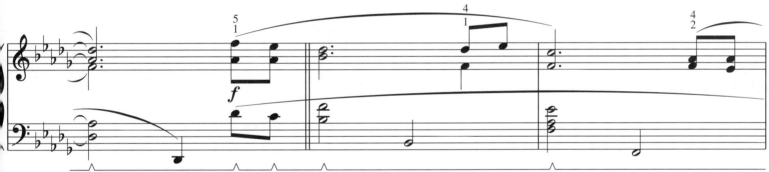

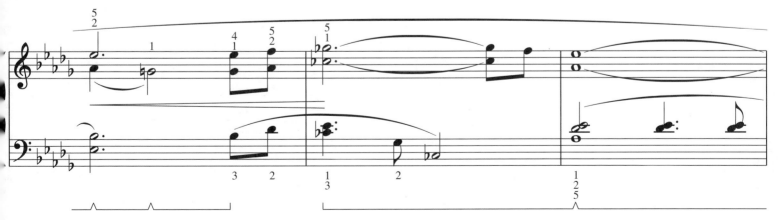

16

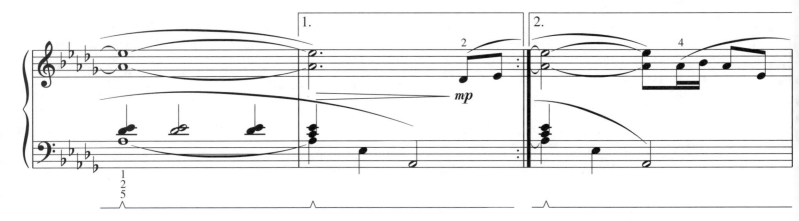

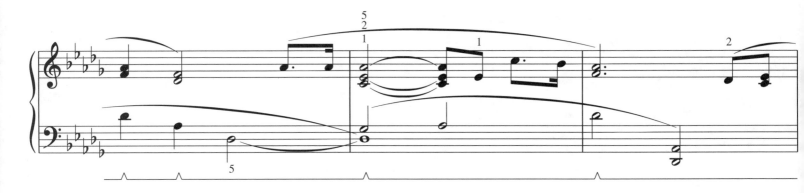

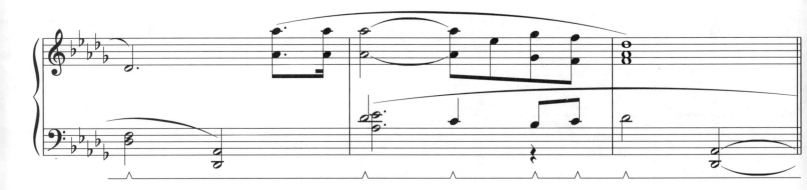

17

(Interlude)

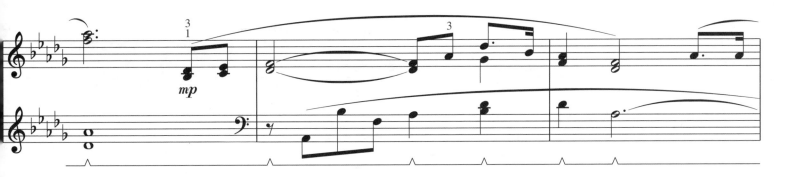

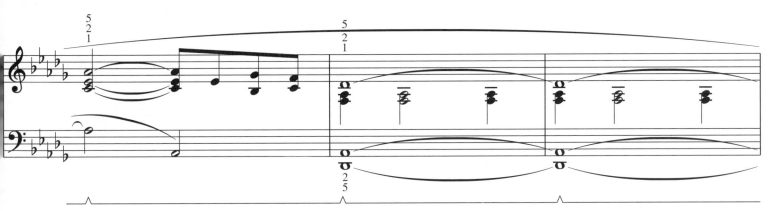

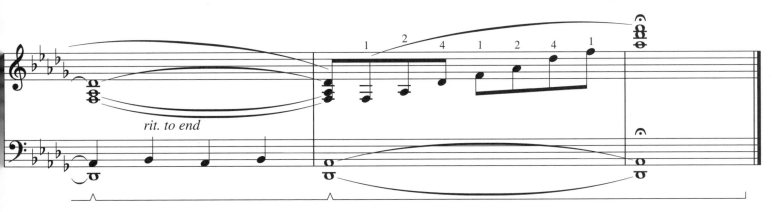

rit. to end

THY WORD

Words and Music by MICHAEL W. SMITH
and AMY GRANT
Arranged by LEE EVANS

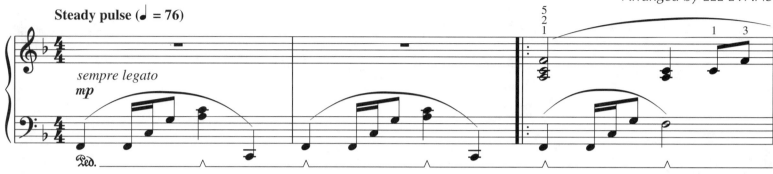

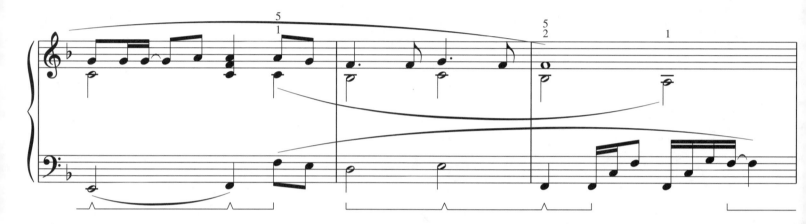

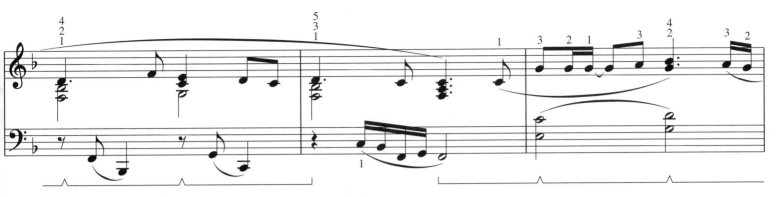

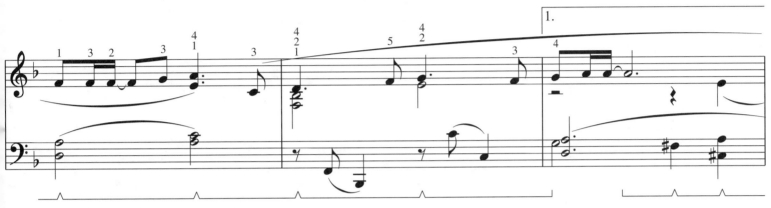

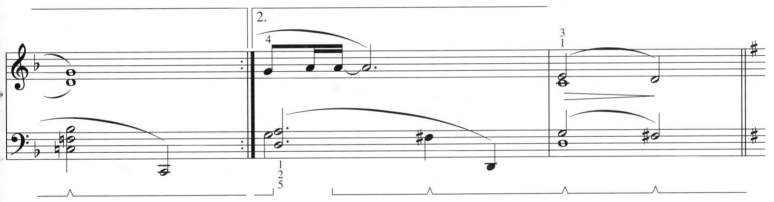

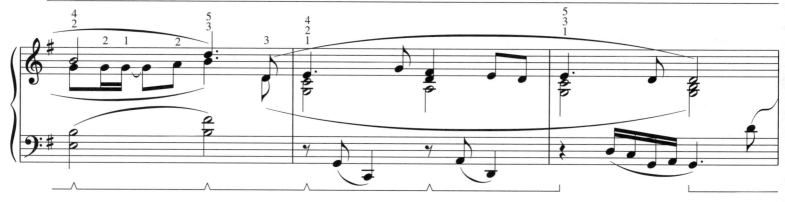

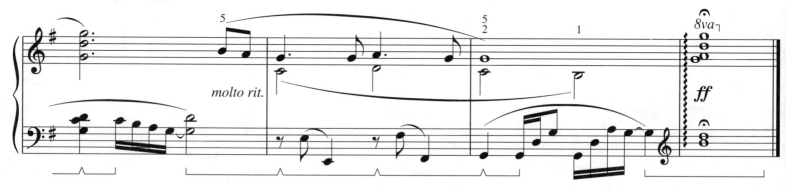

WE WILL GLORIFY

Words and Music by
TWILA PARIS
Arranged by LEE EVANS

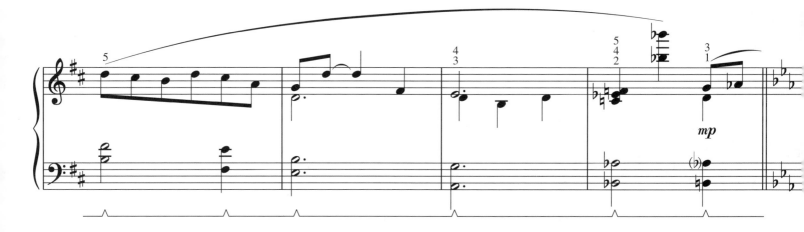

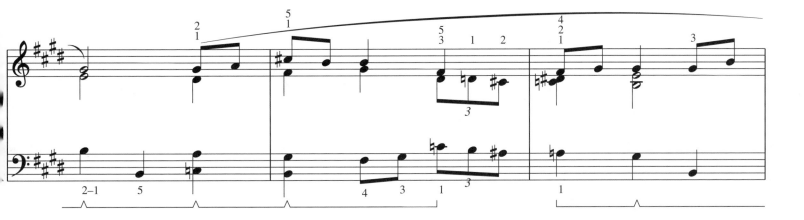

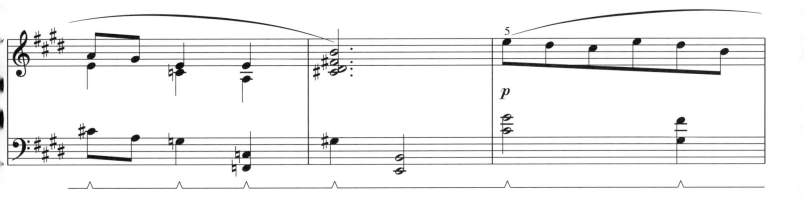

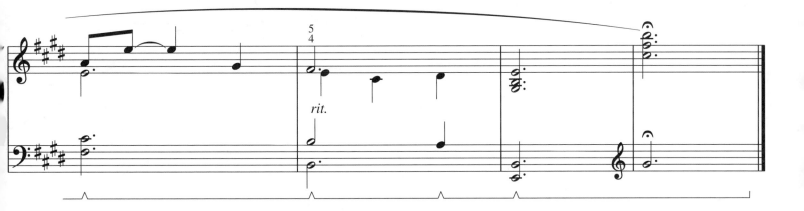

AWESOME GOD

Words and Music by
RICH MULLINS
Arranged by LEE EVANS

Moderate rock feel (♩ = 88)

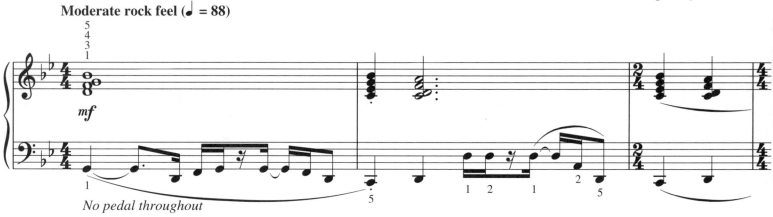

No pedal throughout

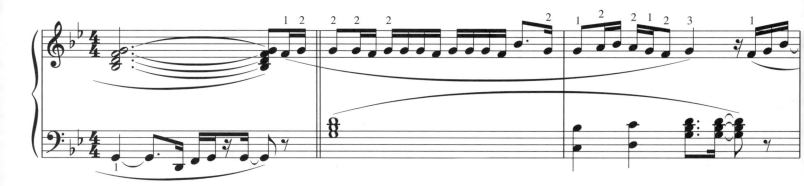

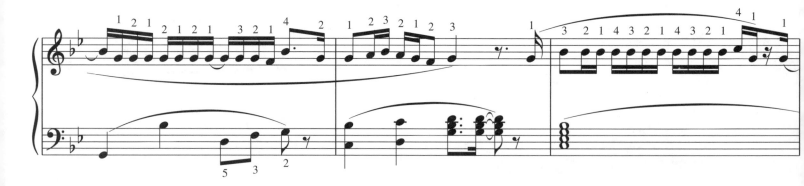

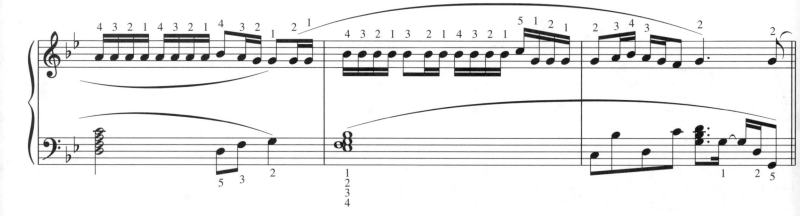

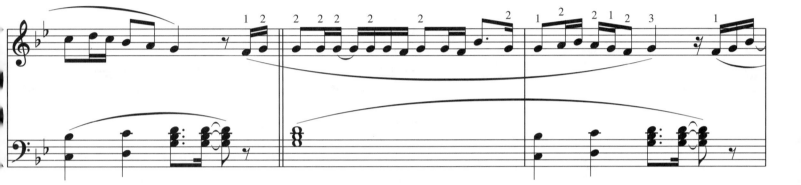

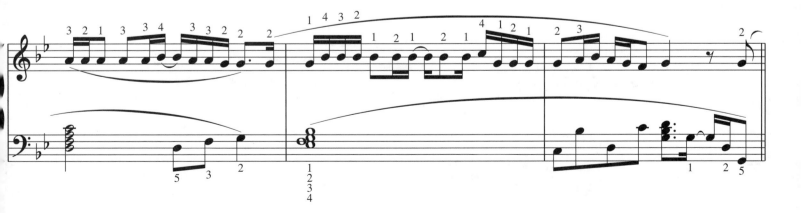

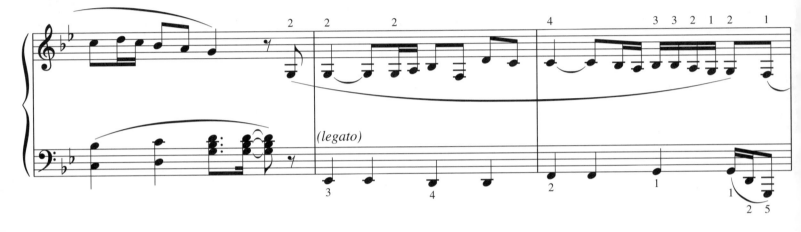

(legato)

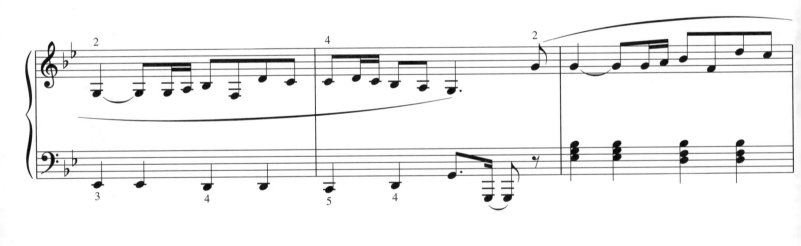

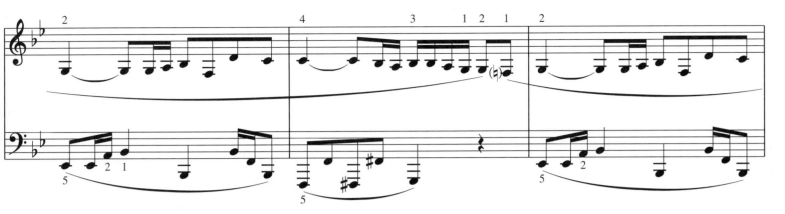

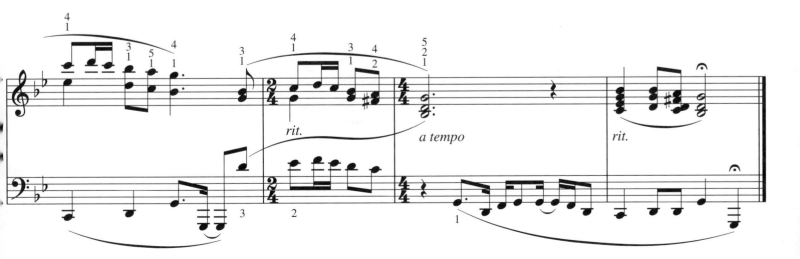

THE MISSION

Words and Music by RANDALL DENNIS
and JON MOHR
Arranged by LEE EVANS

With fervor (♩ = 66)

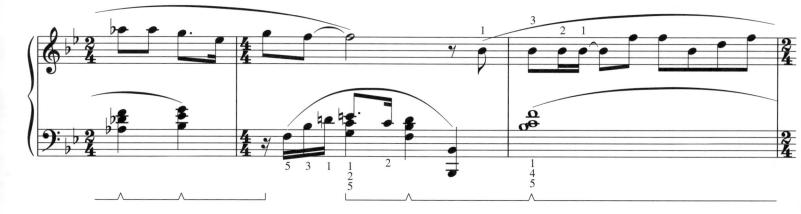

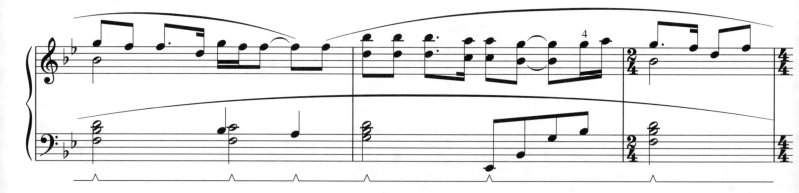

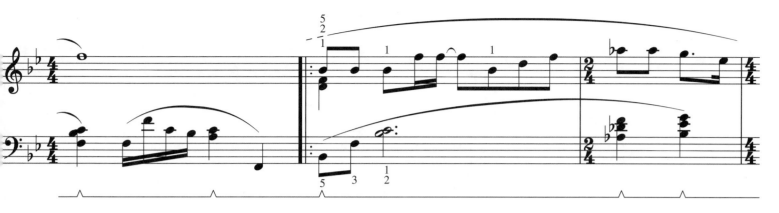

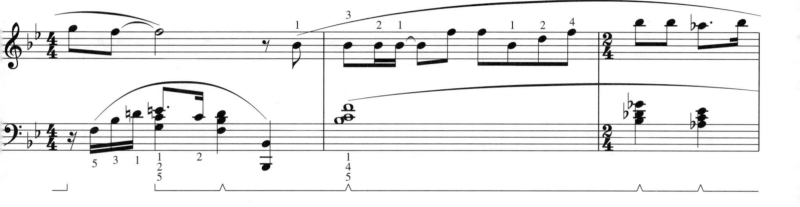

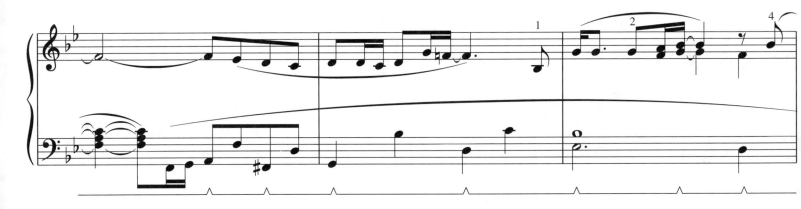

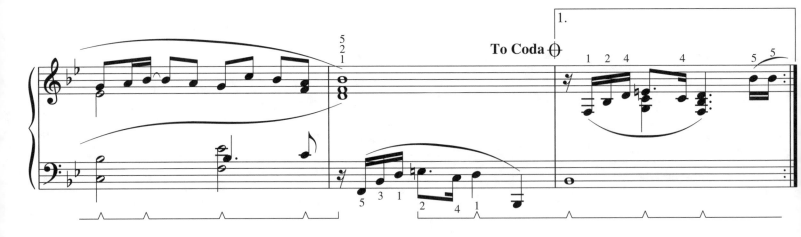

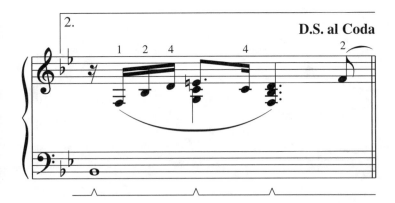

MY TURN NOW

Words and Music by STEVEN CURTIS CHAPMAN
and BRENT LAMB
Arranged by LEE EVANS

With spirit (♩ = 138) (♫ played as ♩♪)

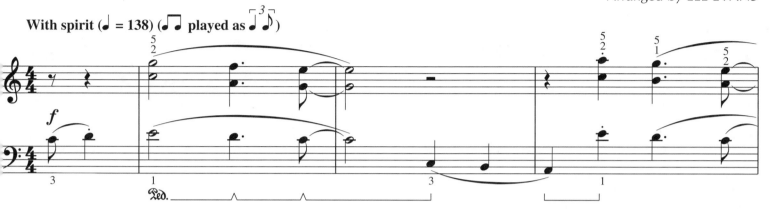

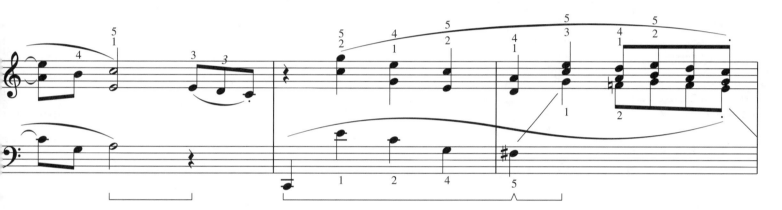

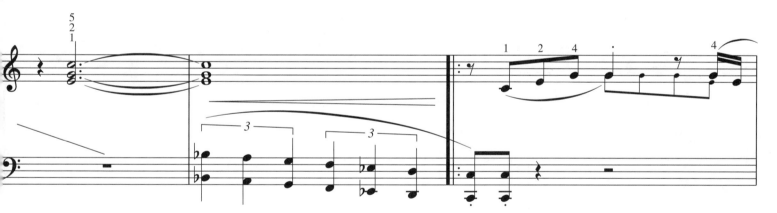

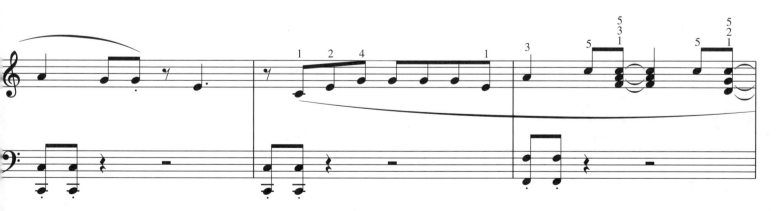

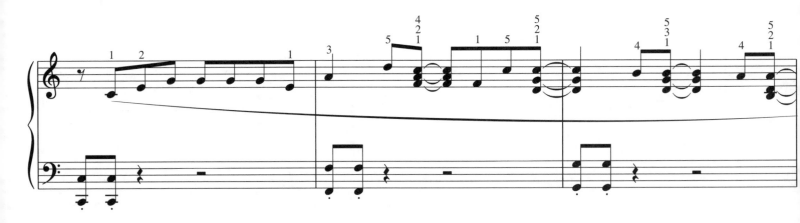

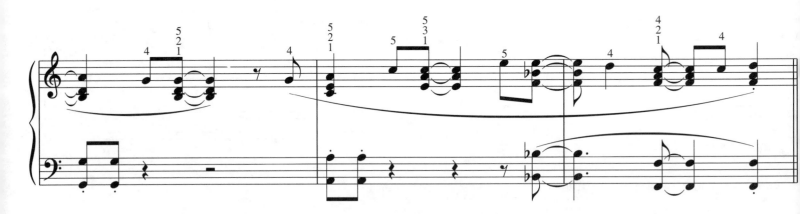

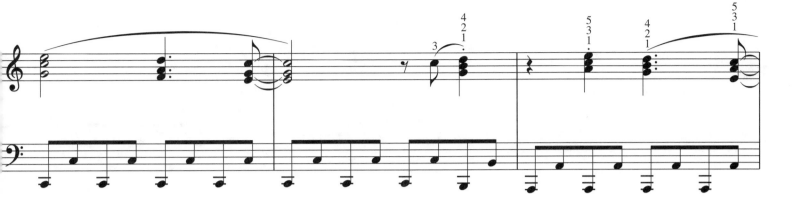

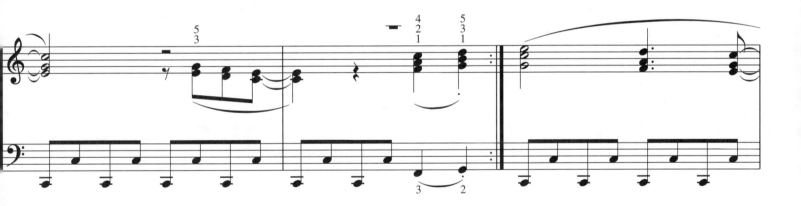

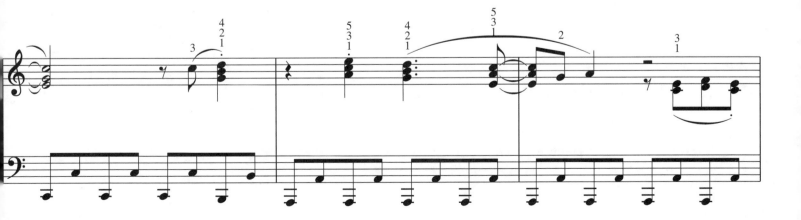

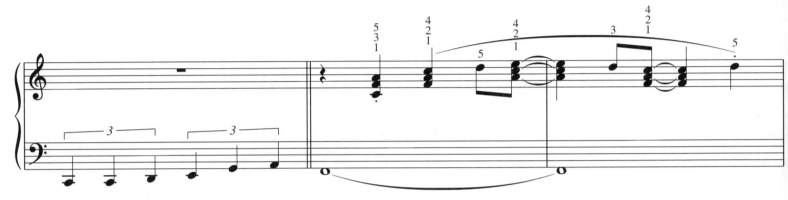

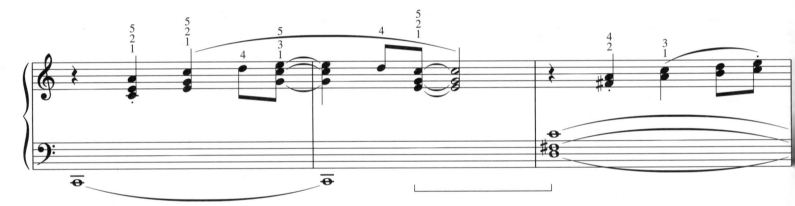

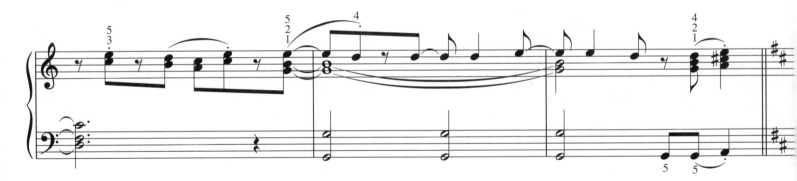

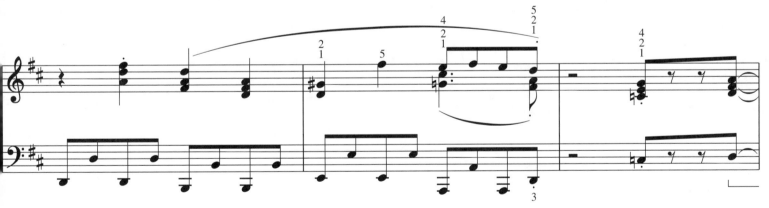

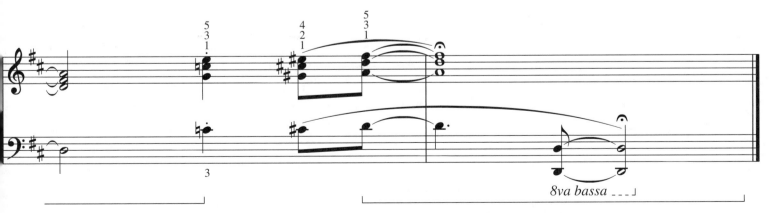

8va bassa _ _ _ _ _

EMBRACE THE CROSS

Words and Music by
JOHN G. ELLIOTT
Arranged by LEE EVANS

Moderately; gently (circa ♩ = 72)

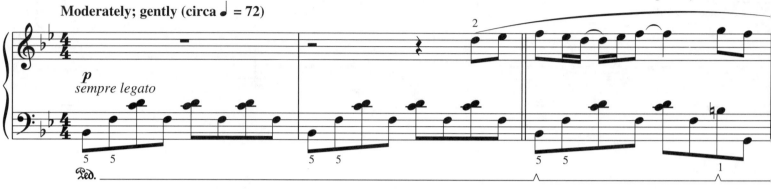

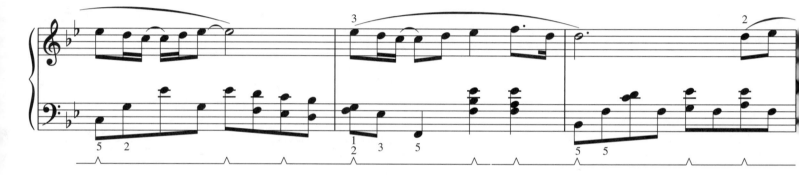

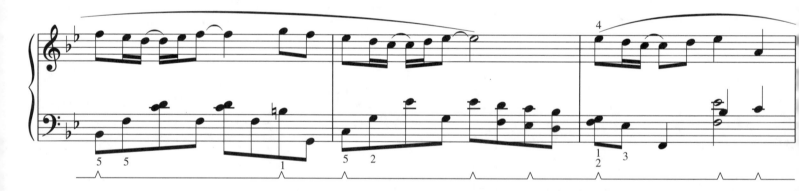

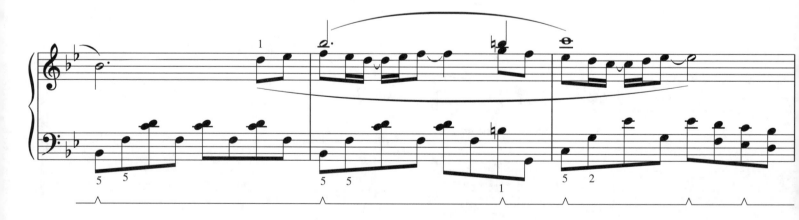

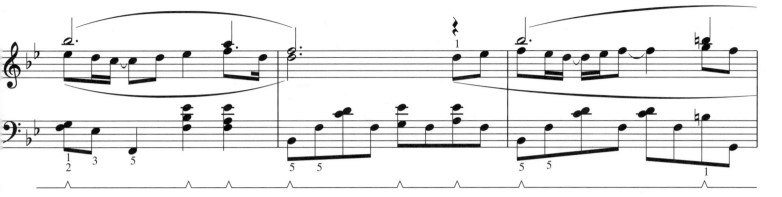

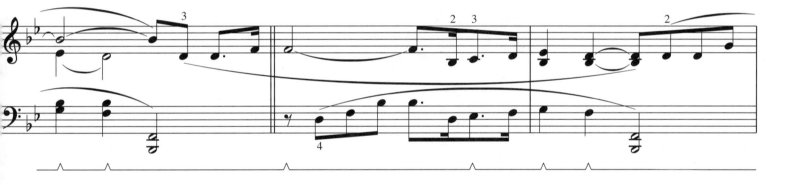

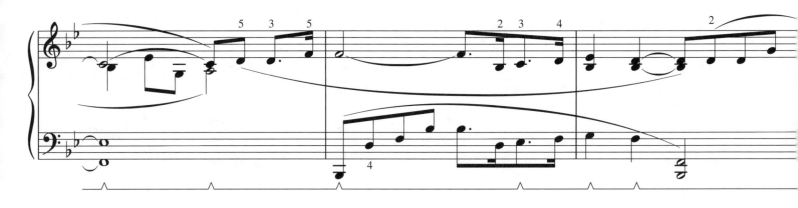

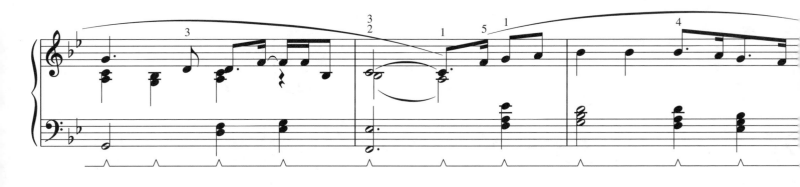

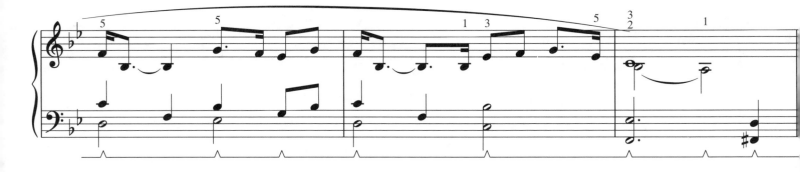

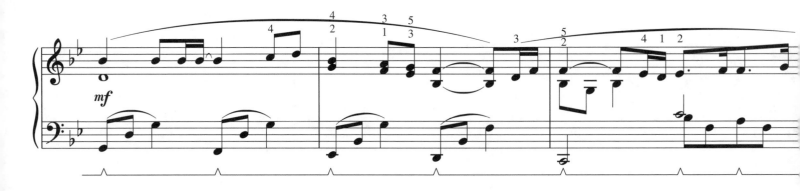

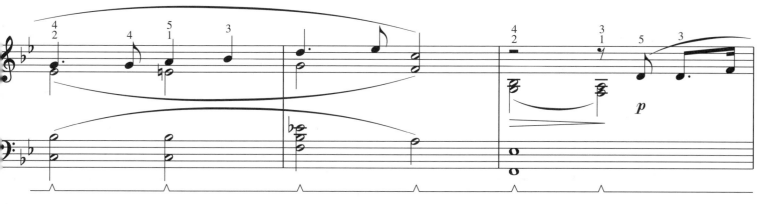

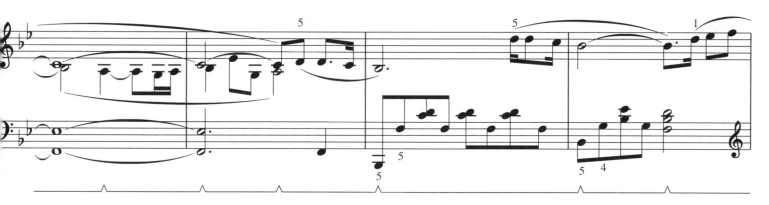

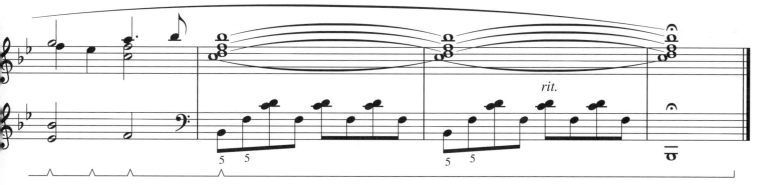

THANK YOU

Words and Music by
RAY BOLTZ
Arranged by LEE EVANS

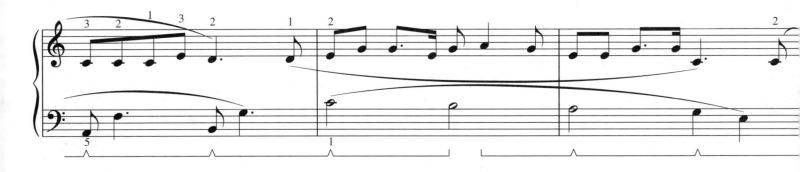

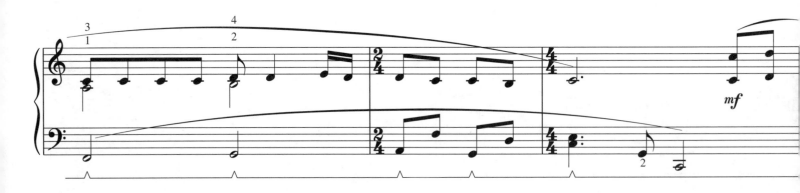

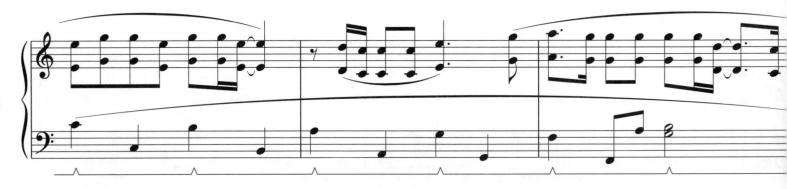

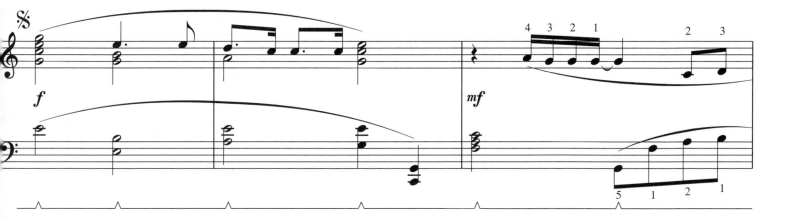

To Coda ⊕

D.S. al Coda

CODA
⊕

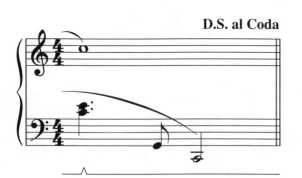

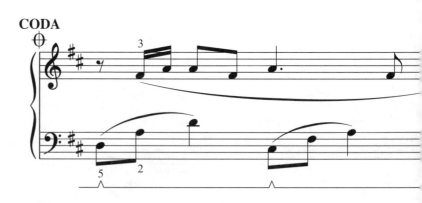

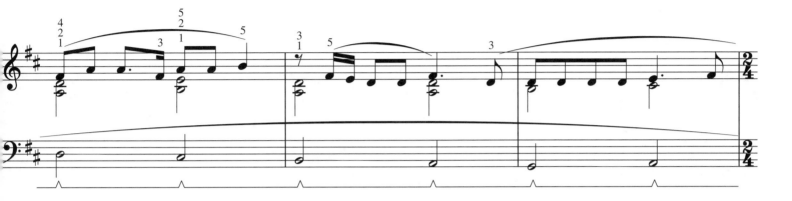

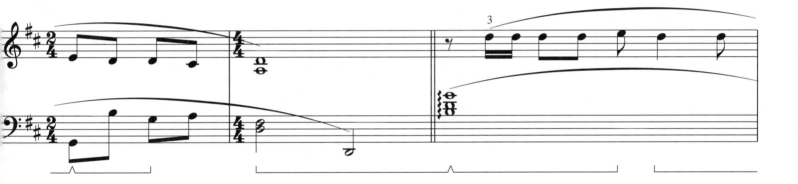

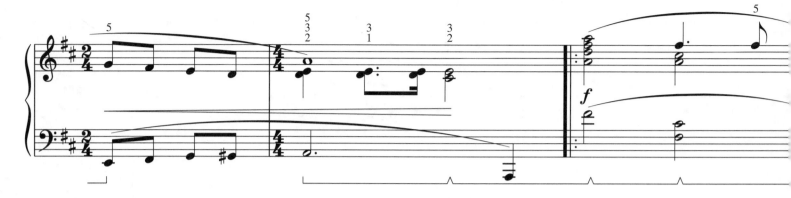

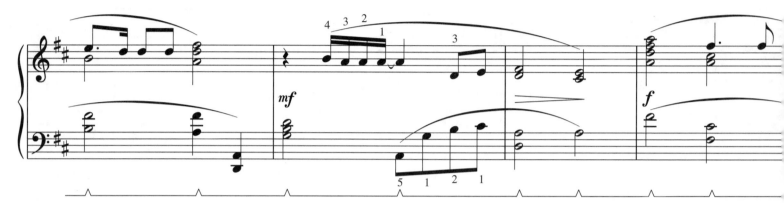

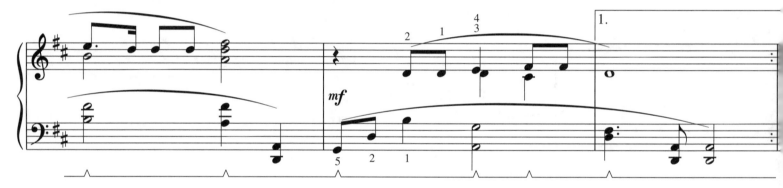

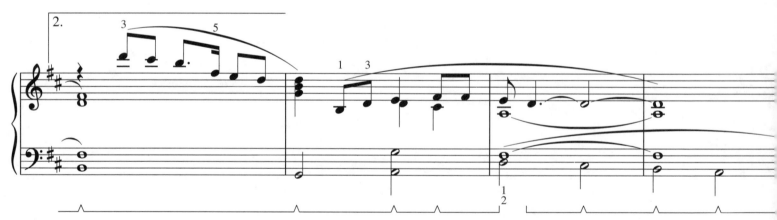

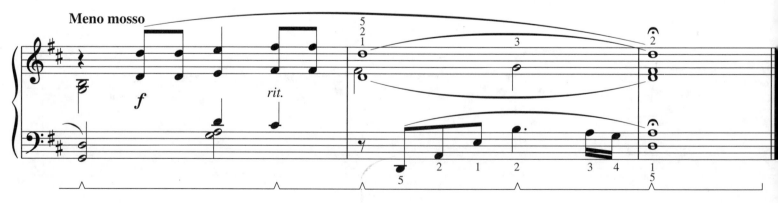

IN CHRIST ALONE

Words and Music by DON KOCH
and SHAWN CRAIG
Arranged by LEE EVANS

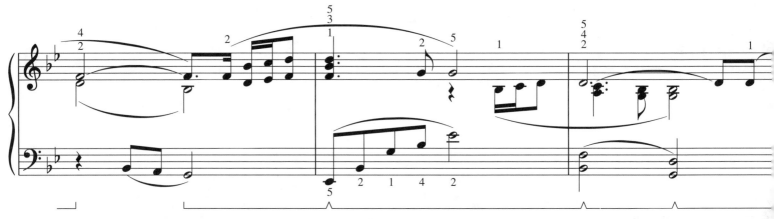

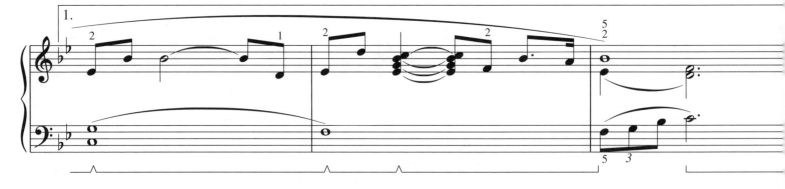

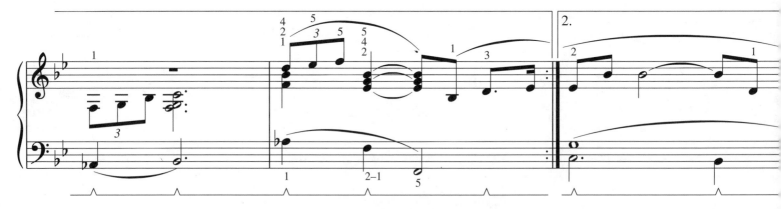

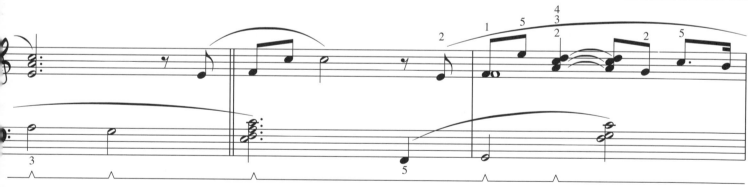

molto rit.

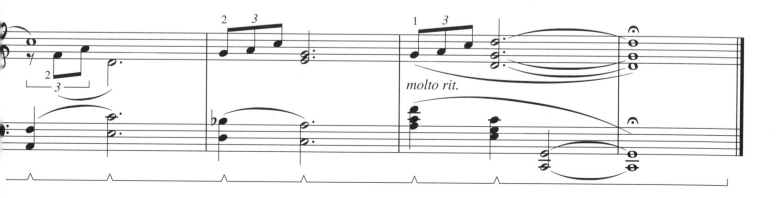

LEE EVANS ARRANGES PIANO SOLOS

Lovely harmonic settings of twelve moving contemporary Christian favorites, arranged for piano by Lee Evans.

HL00290600

LEE EVANS ARRANGES Inspirational Songs
INCLUDING: All My Trials, Nobody Knows The Trouble I've Seen, What A Friend We Have In Jesus, Just A Closer Walk With Thee, Give Me That Old Time Religion and more for PIANO SOLO

Hal Leonard Publishing Corporation

LEE EVANS ARRANGES CONTEMPORARY CHRISTIAN FAVORITES
INCLUDING: Awesome God • Calvary's Love • How Beautiful • Majesty • and more for PIANO SOLO!

HAL•LEONARD®

LEE EVANS ARRANGES BEAUTIFUL HYMNS AND SPIRITUALS

HE Hal Leonard Publishing Corporation

Lee Evans Arranges Inspirational Songs. 11 tasteful piano solos in a completely new and delightful Lee Evans musical perspective.

HL00009085

Lee Evans Arranges Beautiful Hymns and Spirituals. New interpretations of 12 of the world's most beautiful hymns and spirituals ever written.

HL00009635

U.S. $8.95

ISBN 0-7935-6822-6

0 73999 29300 5

HL00290600

HAL•LEONARD®